AF342710

by KENNETH IRBY

The Roadrunner (1964)

Kansas — New Mexico (1965)

Movements / Sequences (1965)

The Flower of Having Passed Through Paradise in a Dream (1968)

Kenneth Irby

* * * * * * * * * * * * *

RELATION

* * * * * * * * * * * * *

Poems 1965 - 1966

Black Sparrow Press
Los Angeles 1970

Copyright © 1970
by Kenneth Irby

ACKNOWLEDGEMENT

My thanks to the following publications, and their editors, where some of
these poems (sometimes in differing versions) first appeared: *Poetry* (Henry
Rago); *Wild Dog* (Drew Wagnon); *Work* (John Sinclair); *Poems Now* (Hettie
Jones); *Io* (Richard Grossinger).

SBN: 87685-013-1 (paper)

     87685-014-X (limited cloth)

For Larry Goodell, Robert Kelly, and Lowell Levant —
friends, poets, loved ones,
sustainers of the spirit

TABLE OF CONTENTS

PREFACE

I have denied all of these poems, in one way or another, at one time or another — and have also recognized that they are as much *me*, the forces through me, as any other act or notion of myself I have. The poems are survivals, then, as Walter Prescott Webb said of the Great Plains, *The land itself is a survival.*

*

Most of these poems were written in Berkeley, California; some also in San Francisco and Palo Alto; and others in Placitas, New Mexico, Lawrence, Kansas, and Princeton, New Jersey. So I was, in these two years, over and over at the concerns of travel (outward or inward) and domesticity — Nuñez' *Relación* and Coleridge's "Frost at Midnight"; Haniel Long and Martin Buber; James C. Malin and George MacDonald's *Lilith;* Edward Dorn's *Geography* and Robert Duncan's *A Book of Resemblances* — as I am still in them.

*

Being homeless, I was given a home by these friends: Sam Spencer; Pat and Michael Abramovitz; Mary and Michael Yeaton; Jerry Aistrup; Martha and Alan Kimball; Thisbe and Don Blake; John Friedman; Edward Grier; Larry Goodell; Angela and James Irby; my parents. Without them I could hardly have survived at all.

*

The *pastoral,* as a mode of poetry (out of the eight Sir Philip Sidney lists), seemed to me particularly of two concerns: a calmness, a quietude of the whole being, derived from all attentions and awareness; and a feeling of great closeness with the vegetation lived among — an ecological calm — poetry that *feeds* us (*pascere*), not just that tends the sheep. I know Pasternak (his Zhivago, that is) concluded that the pastoral nowadays is an artificial genre, a falsity, for *the living language of our time . . . is the language of urbanism.* It seems to me that classical pastoral verse was always the product of city dwellers hankering back to an idealized rustic simplicity (as Bruno Snell, for example, discusses the process in the last chapter of his *The Discovery of the Mind*), and thus the mode was, strictly speaking, always "artificial." But I am concerned here with the precise landscape wherever we are, here and now, as the "spiritual landscape." What plants grow in my backyard, 1614½ A Russell, Berkeley, California; and how I am aware of them. For the pastoral mode, as I feel it, enacts a state of consciousness or awareness, eternally and recurringly common to human beings, every day, every life. Given the amount of shit we live in, it is also manure for all manner of living growth.

The cherry and plum trees are in bloom again, spring come unbelievably early for a man such as myself, born and raised in the plains. A great lushness of the sclerophyllous landscape, and an accumulation of all our humours. As the land arouses the sensuality, so the corruption of the earth exasperates and frustrates, a hoarseness of the loins. The soft, green Berkeley hills hang down almost into Sproul Plaza, where once again strikers, for the same old silly *(selig)* demands of respect and the word, are beaten and tear-gassed by the cops. The irascible longing. There is always a poignancy, living here in California, in this land that should have been the most beneficent of all human dwelling-places. The poetry of this mild littoral clime is marked by many turnings, distracted and multiplied attentions — but centrally, in my own case, by the conviction that the landscape demands us, and reveals us.

Berkeley
Feb-Mar 69

RELATION

Poems 1965-1966

There is no illusory world, there is only the world.

— MARTIN BUBER

the correspondence of natural things with spiritual things, or of the world with heaven, is through uses, and uses are what conjoin

— EMMANUEL SWEDENBORG

A true account of the actual is the rarest poetry

— H. D. THOREAU

JANUARY 1965, LOOKING ON

Moss in the gratings
of a sewer vent

And past me have gone
a lady cop in a yellow slicker
ticketing in the rain
and those who have come in and out
after books

There is no image the flesh
does not take in, sink, the hook, there is
a weight beyond me all afternoon, into the drizzle
uncertainties of
how to look

A man comes in selling ballpoint pens
"I won't be back to bother you for a long time, not till April —
I'll let you have all three for 75¢ — they all write"

And in the dust on the floor of that used-book store?
So seared, the scars he must have had so long
any look back at him
is not even felt?

Moss
on the sewer plates

And on Clement Street
leads straight to the Pacific
men dead on their feet
come — back? home? down hard —
to die. The clod prim slickered copess

And there is no footprint
no print in the moss
the wet, sopped weeks of rain
does not take out of men, bodies
the bodies sopped
staining the filthy concrete

The rancors of texts and elucidations

And the quiet light down on the dust, in the windows, in this store

My God, my hands stuffed in my dirty pockets

11 Jan 65

TWO FRAGMENTS FOR BILL DODD

The loneliness of West Texas
as Ed Dorn said, like the love of death

"the loneliness," the man had
cattlemen came on, wandering east of Las Vegas, in the Staked
                                                        Plains

was not of the people missing
but of the endless eventless landscape

where what few rises there are
give only onto the same repeated vista as before

and to be born there
is what you look for, out any gaze

and the stretch clear on through
out the back of the head

*

Tulia
Mule Shoe
Dimmitt
Floydada
Levelland
Plainview
Whiteface
Meadow
Crosbyton
Spur
Lamesa
Bovina
Friona
Paducah
Dawn
Goodnight

                                        12 Jan 65

It is almost 2 months since I have seen you
                Where the body can touch them
Light out in Berkeley is behind clouds only
                Geraniums
The least parts of the body thrive
                As into this light
Out to meet the great
                Do I go completely
The 3 circles of the stupa in the brain
                Into the fields there, S. Folsom St., the pastures
                                where you wander

Morning lecture after, walking in the rain
                Out, past where I am
Puddles, carved urns, barbed wire
                Are what I carry with me
Maybeck's gymnasium for women
                Out, past these windows
I have not seen you anywhere
                There is so little love, I mean
I have only wanted to see you everywhere
                At 5 a.m. and dawn on
Visits to San Francisco, the surly unemployment dirt
                I have awakened into the same light as all day long
                                today
Even at 2 a.m. you were not at home
                Gordon come, on to Los Angeles, not stayed
Gordon come, on to Los Angeles, not stayed
                Even at 2 a.m. you were not at home
I have awakened into the same light as all day long today
                Visits to San Francisco, the surly unemployment dirt
At 5 a.m. and dawn on
                I have only wanted to see you everywhere
There is so little love, I mean
                I have not seen you anywhere
Out, past these windows
                Maybeck's gymnasium for women
Are what I carry with me
                Puddles, carved urns, barbed wire
Out, past where I am
                Morning lecture after, walking in the rain
Into the fields there, S. Folsom St., the pastures where you wander

                    The 3 circles of the stupa in the brain
Do I go completely
                    Out to meet the great
As into this light
                    The least parts of the body thrive
Geraniums
                    Light out in Berkeley is behind clouds only
Where the body can touch them
                    It is almost 2 months since I have seen you

                                                    30 Mar 65

I am so tired tonight I cannot even see past this room
        into the next dark room, look up, focus to look there
past the map of Kansas look
remember any my old pictures of
old times last night too drunk to drive home
would I enter the wood desk, lie flat, return

o open gold
                bottle of elixir
fragile of one headlight busted and burned out and the left front
                                                tire shot

the arguments got into tonight with old friends
know better, I don't
                    ram me head on
out the window at dark
                        night wet lights from across the bay
and the talk still going on
                    quiet let sights drum no loss be day
                                        from each other

in the kitchen

                    Here may I chew my cud
                     it will be time to sleep
                     soon enough let no
                     zap slip through
                       untouched
                       the fingers

*

So he's walking up & down all whichaway this & that jiggly
and this man come out the woodwork, cabinet, file drawers,
                                        green eyeshade
white spats old gold studs a roll two hole & three up turn down
                                            the corners
the eye lights & looks straight shot at him, roll me no cigarettes
                            I'll light you no butts
        would I hang loose ends my sweet song along time
        never no ways & anyhow flipped up the pencil caught it
        wondered where to go & called it putting the piece

back in shape:

—of the hand
—to do the required exercises
—Supreme Headquarters Allied Powers in Europe

now falls the memory to,
the flow of,
unhinge

"To quiet the mind and make it receptive to divine influences"

that one may even sleep
and fall like rain

15 Apr 65

THE JOURNEY ITSELF IS HOME

— BASHŌ

That is the mind's trip
anywhere
            as well as roads forever never settled
stretch

            If I do not come to rest
            in me
there is no home not of the mind
more peace

            Stations, way
            places toward
            the relish in
            all things

            the stretch out
            toward that
            —entrance—
            resolution
            that is the
            mind's peace
            love

*

Am I willing to be lost?
                        that is
a way as well

lost, is fuckup of the choice made,
realized? arrogance of intention, that we *knew*
from here? shown
vanity

            When there is
            no way
            that is not
            arbitrary in
            some other way,
            we stumble on

            and survival comes back
            to ourselves
            who have so fought
            to rule

                          2 May 65

FREEDOM IS THE UNCLOSING OF THE IDEA WHICH LIES
                              AT OUR ROOT:
THE FREEDOM OF THE ROSE TREE IS THE ROSE.

— GEORGE MACDONALD

the flow of vegetation
        to know dissections of
                is not to enter

its flow —
                I would not impose
upon, myself upon,
                but sit here in the yard, the continuities,
out of myself, into the sun, back again,
into the tangles of wisteria, the heavy smell,
the rhododendron bush alone, nasturtiums
up beside the dilapidated summer house, spread lawn
notched by bushes (camelia) of this yellow Victoria
's age's house, and where I sit the cottage behind
on Bonita St., Berkeley
                        opens us all to the bay

                we strive
            into around
            each other

*

and on the bed inside, Mary asleep
        who lay asleep against me all night
                after, where, we intertwined

and in this house look at each other smiling
        lit in the open shade, clear day
                is our open month the May

may all times for us however short together
        be — open, light — around us
                wet in each other, wet all over each other

23

as wet spray as the sprinkler Mr. Street
        runs where looks on off any look
                the bay lies, "sheeten metal," Michael said a day ago
                it is today
                                and seeds our air
                                with its endless wet

*

I mean, Mary, I enter you and I look on now
as I wake up, move
from my tangles
knots darks and shifts where the fence to next door
is so thick with vines only a few boards show
                                into the sun

you have now so opened
        where I lay
                simply to be here, at ease

                        is world walk
                        clomp clomp snick snick
                        lengths of footsteps
                        in the gravel drive

it is past any demand but what we take ourselves
        calm, in us, where we want to go

I grow beside you
        as your wisteria adds silently at night
                minute fractions of an inch

and the fragrance
                        I had forgotten that smell of a woman
we mix
                sounds of the evening approach
                as you wake and move
                the squeaking springs

24

*

blue striped cup   tin pail   beer bottle
blanket spread   red plastic car   gray & yellow plastic truck

the children's aura   left in these   turned upside down
grow in the grass   as we   children in us
grow in the light   falls across   the face

what we have left   grows   behind us

faces in the mirror   swarm   blood in the hand

insects turn the dirt wisteria flowers blow

so heavy your sleep   the breath stirs beside the bed
                          the curtains

3 May 65

THE BRIEF CONNECTION

At another day minus four years I would have been back in the
    barracks, duty ended, locked into the indigenous landscape,
    liquor, listlessness out the window, Albuquerque, set into
    the Army out of time except eventual release —

that long country of flat perspective, and dry, I read of this after-
    noon again, Haniel Long's *Piñon Country* again, running a
    tailor shop in San Francisco, the years and the distance of
    hand to cover whatever land, crossed, matter not as much
    as landscape held in the head and incessantly crisscrossed as
    sunlight's different slant of fall is here down Clay St., half
    a block from Portsmouth Square the Sydney Ducks and
    whorehouses radiated from like spokes of a wheel —

it's the time of day I want a drink — there, from a hidden and
    illegal bottle if I had it, or beer brought back from the Picnic
    House across the street — here, I have sold nothing all day
    (no garters, fat ties, Harris tweed socks) to pay for, finance:
    lost high finances — as if near payday in the Army and
    bereft of ability to drink in company that paid, left to write
    angles in the windows out upon those mountains east —
    tonight I go home to Berkeley — there is the question still
    of cause

18 Aug 65

SEQUENCE

So we wait on the verge of —
                              the want to move on again
The pressure that becomes unbearable to stay in one place any
                                                            longer

American history is the only history

Local history is the only history

            it is the
                      body
        answers

*

P. came in this morning and told me
his wife had been raped Friday night — coming home
drunk from a party they waited over an hour for a bus
and arguing he got mad and walked home by himself — she tried
the people at the party and called a cab, and waiting
3 guys hit her —
                              "after 2 days of eating ourselves
apart over that, we decided to move — to Albuquerque,
Tucson, the SW somewhere like that"

And in the lunchcounter later, drinking coffee,
he talked about George Catlin — *everytime I go east*
I feel I'm going against an enormous tide

*

I'd said when I came to San Francisco, the only way to go east
after you've come this full tilt west to the ocean
is north and then east again — the great
clockwise undercurrents of the continent

But we'll go the south route next month
to Albuquerque to pick up my books that are stored there
and they'll probably go with us

*

That is, what makes us move?
                              This thing
for them —
                they'd been talking about leaving for months,
moving to a new apartment soon, anyway —

this rape

They tend no cattle in the sunned pastures
of these streets, not even a car
what grass flesh milk dessert sustains
past the regurgitation of oneself, and eaten all again?

it is the pressure cooker's lid blown off
of the lady who lived behind us in Fort Scott
her face and arms burned into scars

what dispossesses us
what we do not have to take
        sitting down,
                    but move —

*

All day has been the necessary tedium
        to come to this quiet —
left alone as Mary's gone to pick up Michael
        and lost in Melville lost into *Clarel* —
put again by your phonecall
        upon the turn we move upon, where
pivot us, old throaty night quiet songs
        before we leave, tell us
where we've lived, here, sweaty
        drawers left, garbage sacks thrown out the window —

    Mary come home asks me to take the garbage out
    and in the yard the amaryllis' smell is thick, their pink —
    so soft they turn in the dark yard the stamens clink
    filter butts in the grass thrown out of the upstairs window
        roll cold against my feet

28

The important question of our movement
is how different it is to go this in & out I have tonight
and you to move that move to come to Albuquerque

— to come to this quiet

even Michael's shouts and machinegun rasps
do not disturb, garbage sacks or clock ticks

is from or to that same movement you move on now? all
lost shit necessary first to rest at all? what done
to come to whatever ease, lasts now, while it is, endless — last
fall in isolation on 48th Avenue, wandering Golden Gate Park
where groundhogs came and went and doberman bitches
to greet me, what pain of loving a friend I could not touch,
slow turn up and down night mattresses without, as rose and fell
the geraniums' saturation glow, the fog that came and left

we move, to lose the pain? I moved
to this yard, it took months, it's taken
months to reach this ease tonight —

the difference of the distance of the travel, the length of the steps,
        long time —

and then we wait on the verge of —?

as I wait on any step at all out there in the yard
for the chink, the clink, in the amaryllis, to open
or to begin to bore into —

as you endure the lapsed long pain of *where?*
and a weekend of rape and after eaten into and out again

to face any new place
and rechallenge the power of your roots
        to sink into

Let it come, let it come,
the age of our desire

I have endured so long
I have forgotten everything

23-24 Aug 65

GYMNOPÉDIE

I get up to pee, and you
to take off your clothes in Michael's room, look
after where he lies asleep, come
then and piss after me, and then to bed

lapse into silence
is the night we have not
looked at
except the windows are
so dark
they only show
reflections back

and the moon hangs
gravy heavy
cloud full
in the redwood
shakes
beyond the hedge

day to come
in our fingers
we will fuck
into being

night
in the pit of the stomach
eases

Hangs down,
          Michael,
you start and snort now,
rustles its boughs
wherein the flute plays
carrying on its length
the 12 dancing princesses

lift up their skirts
to pee

31

stains down the walk outside
in yellow glitters
past your eyes

*

Fresh may we wake to
what we have made

7 Sep 65

SERIES — 4 OCT 65

step out this evening to see the constellations
sought nights before and light too light across the sky here,
Berkeley bends toward Oakland and glows, to see — that I wait up
late now till darkened, and at the west horizon
the Scorpio to rise before this month is out, that is my birth's
                                                        sign —
look in the evening before the bay is dark, for the evening star,
Venus, come into the house where whips his tail
my sign, my flesh, the opened and then tightened countenance

Anger's movie is of this season?
                        All Hallows' Eve
in the flesh, the sky turn bends to,
                                that in the aftermath of,
November, I was born —
                        may the year leap again
as the child from its mother
                                into the light —
tail coiled and sprung
                        the sharp sting of light
                        to come

*

the house, all houses
to be roofless, then —
the yellow sky that
Stan and Coleridge and Crane
demand, and the stars,
canopy me if I
walk where they open
continually — may I —
for it is all prayer,
that we go past even where
we want to be, fail
at — be so open
that no other
house's roof will do
but this — this

none, this all, this
endless spread of sky

*

acceptance give us, where before there was none
acceptance, even before we can love —
if I came down onto the bed to you
and we fucked the whole afternoon — sweat rises from,
mist now at dark, drifts through the eucalyptus on the hills
east toward Orinda, west along the bay,
what we have given back into nature
as taken — it is the anger yesterday, shout
and I called you every kind of bitch as you sat on the toilet
trying to piss, Michael between us —
come back, opened up and split open, talked about,
into some ease, some, whatever little, taking of us
as we are — acceptance, acceptance give us,
even before we can love — living together, live together,
where before there was none

quiet as you sleep now
the gas hisses in the stove, and the moon
covers into blue the empty beer cans on the porch

*

so we have lived together here five months now — the yard become
our courtyard, our portico of the sky's covering

the major portents are
arrivals past the hedge and garage:
        Frosty the white samoyed
        friends
        the landlord in bib overalls

*

in the flesh the flower blooms
of the freeway from Oakland to the Bay Bridge
and off it toward Emeryville three vacant lots like parade fields

eucalyptus still grow in along one side

is in the hand turning the tub's faucet
water out, as the cars' flow on the freeway,
in fits and jerks before it runs, twistings
of the vine's stem, before
the flower's come to, and the tendrils
turned in upon, out around
where the light falls

as I turn to you in the dark turned away from me in bed
cup my crotch to your buttocks, flatten my hand
across your stomach
the flower bursts
the petals flow as moving lines between the skins
along the ridges where the sweat is
into bloom

canopied flower, skin
full of stars, yellow
light shining
back into our eyes
the gloss of eucalyptus leaves
our loving's fetor
reeks of

and shakes, trembles
in the winds
as leaves, as curtains
at our windows

*

and the portents that come, lead away:
— the landlord who snoops,
    mowing the grass in the morning looks in the windows,
    and won't let us stay
— the white snow dog
    who endlessly wants to go away, anywhere, waits,

lies sleeping beside the car so no one
can leave without him knowing
— the friends, already moved,
John and Gail gone

they are so literal, the signs —
        tides, ephemeral, go far away

4 Oct 65

MOON

We have entered the dark stretch of night just before dawn
as we have entered the dark stretch of land
before the home's come to

It is not anywhere an ease of meeting anyone we come upon
distrust is natural as want of companions
and we who have entered into such closeness with the land
less and less crave anyone

I have said, "O Moon, my wife!" and again tonight
as the moon is full over the imagined, fabled city
the pitches of the body are turned to her, are hers

"Rich weeds!" Only the treed and then blank land
is city for us — to approach the western mountains
hold stones of moon as promise — but she dwells here
spread upon the grass, to plow into
our cocks as shares to turn the earth
sweat and come, light and light
sink into, planted here

What noises we have heard in the night
are those who guard her jealously

We come
new
to wed her

*

That is what the dream tells, wide awake
under the full moon has risen an hour ago
over San Francisco — I am in the fabled city
and the mind goes backwards into Kansas, come there
naked and tired and two hundred years ago, new
and explorer of the plains
home came to be —
                        there are no dreams of now
                        there were not then — to push

                    into the new land
                    was not to plant there
                    new cities like the old
                    in every heart — as I
                    have wedded in the time old thoughts
                    the moon in full tonight
                    did they
                    who came there first

*

In the back Tim and Jerry are building on the new room
The chair I sit in is a camp chair. The beer is Colt 45
The ground the self can see at all now
is so complicated, so many levels, so thick
conglomerate, so dense the trees
I do not even know the names of —

                              may then the welter
                              of such facts the gaps cannot
                              snap and crackle fast enough
                              to hold — give way
                              into such ease, the face
                              lets smile, even the back of
                                        the head
                              rests and lets the breath out
                              easily —

Jerry came in and left the stapler
There is the moon
's light around his head

The painting of a wheatfield in South Dakota
lapses from its sunlight
into this moon

We have approached the fact of this land
as body as alive as our own

and then seen beyond us
into the ground
is simpler —

    In the moonlight
    the explorers have lost
    all sense of self

8 Nov 65

Now may the light
night sky bend down with rain
into the cups of our sleeping heads
dreams make us into days of ease

There is not fought a war
we are not in lost in
looking for light moments even one moment
the ease from makes

There is no pain the photograph's pain
may make us equal to
only our own to come to
not hatred but the flowered march

The burn of self outside a union
no one is in but to burn beyond
the face out of
consumes to light

Night sky bend down
that no particle of all
you cover be lost —
excoriated   burned   shot open

Where our heads like cups
wait
where the fire waits
for what day of ease
dreams
do not make

20 Oct 65

What colors are there
in your hair?
                I didn't see
past the red, gone brown
by dark, red hairs around
your cunt — that is the word
we said quietly
in the dark, cock, hard, come
not quietly, but to
quiet
            The long filaments of hair,
of us spun thin into the air, yours
I still find stuck in books, mine
are with you, all over the house?
Bind us
            Your hair, your red
and russet hair, fair winds in the dark
never desert us, the air
of Bach's suite lifts gently
in Palo Alto toward the night slips
west toward the ocean, as east
toward Berkeley and your sleep
the earth turns, runs
before the sun

We who fucked night after night
linked the earth to earth,
                    I think
we made the sun rise
for us, day after day —

the hair, the red
lights of strands

last to

11 Dec 65

41

Dream Children — A Reverie, Lamb called his discursion
into the darkness beyond the lamp, into the back
calm and always present regret — regret   regret
lost intentions colored in the cardboard paper book
at the edges of the room. They recede from him
as he tells
              how it was to be a child himself
to himself —
              We are in a dark room
and the children gone to bed now
are my friend's, not mine — and the road stones' glitter
is golden in the half light toward their bedrooms,
footsteps on as we would go there in our thoughts
or they have already gone on, the marks
of their small feet cut in the gold bricks.
                            Recede from us,
recede from me among my friends
lending me without knowing their eternity.

9 Dec 65

42

RELATION

Mesas, erosion —
who was it, Dutton, Hayden, Gilbert, or Powell, said, it was
the *least* eroded country in America? The rest
all more worn down, long ago, to a nubbin —

Bryce's "hell of a place to lose a cow in" canyon
rims its ampitheater open toward the south
the river there, way south, roads its way
toward lower California, sawn —

    the year the fathers rallied
    round the bell in Philadelphia

    the fathers west crossed
    the crossing of the fathers
    now silt and muddy water
    backed up over the whole long canyon

    toward the home
    stretch, through
    Moquis and Navajos
    toward Albuquerque

    having circled north from Taos
    into the Colorado gorges, west
    through the Uintas, south along the Wasatch
    and across
           looking for California
           and the way thither

* The sun is out here in Palo Alto, and the flame red pyracantha
  clacks its berries against the clapboards, windblown
  as the clouds blown simultaneously show and recover
  the direct sun
            such elements as only lately
            eroded those flats and ranges
            — the "Plateau Province" Powell called it

It takes such soft wool

as Escalante and his fathers wore, such
pain and ease among, such
care to even see
                    to live in that land

                    — on any land, the care, that the wear
                    is of our feet across
                    not inundations planned

Cabeza de Vaca and Escalante
went through the trek, into the land traversed, the heavy
foot lift, over old and used again tracks —
            Sauer and Hallenbeck traced the trails Nuñez used, still
            visible and followable today, from the Texas shore
            to the Guadalupe and Sacramento mountains,
            south along the road to Cíbola —

through the land
is its own experience, care for
what care the land demands

And the interior distance,
the brain pan, the heaviness there

                        — for Escalante only came back
                        where he had begun, a great
                        circle without touching
                                        California
                        or that western sea —

the plains in the mind
eroded to the Ground
the self lost on off
in those steep and wandering canyons

while the soft wool robes, the soft
touch of the
hand of the
naked bearded
wanderer
            created them anew
            who touched

21 Dec 65

The yard of the house at the corner is full of oranges
A dwarf lives there — as in the fairy story
lived under an orange tree, his skin orange —
as here it is his wife, or mistress,
who is orangey

      Don't let your deal go down

      I love the gamblin' man

      O Lord, honey, take a drink on me
      • • •
      Two old maids a-sittin' in the sand
      Each one wishin' the other was a man

But the orange tree is in no desert, as it was
with the other dwarf —
     but here is on
the eastern slope of the coastal range, toward
the south end of San Francisco Bay, whoever lives here
who does not have to, has money —
but the backyard of my friend, a teacher,
is full of what richnesses other climates
aspire to with wealth and ostentation —
lemons, gardenias, pomegranates, roses
in December

This is what we came west for

But I have come south from San Francisco
for these friends. Here it is the day after Christmas
and we listen to the New Lost City Ramblers
waiting for the chickens stuffed with peaches and mushrooms
to cook —

    west along the ridges separating
Palo Alto and Los Altos from the ocean, through
the redwoods at La Honda, down those then open
and now with rain green round valleys
toward the ocean, the afternoon drive
uncovers the land from its piss-ass tracts and highlines

and brings us the old closenesses again
— stopped in some drivein in the last noonmeal of summer —
heights again, they are anew, a new
and other order, kids crying and hollering in the back seat,
get out to pee by the ocean, sand flats awash, a plover on —
& other order, as if it all
were all a new and never come to
meeting of each other, finding ourselves
suddenly among such people
we could love, could face
all shit and waste against us
and survive
into yet another order
of the closeness we had found

*

It is an orange tree the kid there
plummets with oranges to shake down —
past the dwarf and that dark, orange-brown mistress,
his tow head beside the pyracantha berries' red
turns toward the other corner, where two
teenage kids are married, out in the yard working on their car

Rain tonight
and in the morning the streets awash, the sun comes out
as it was yesterday
we said we'd run and laugh in
naked

26 Dec 65

ROSE STREET—JANUARY 1966

Now it flowers,
                    the car out in the street,
the black Volkswagen with the right rear tire flat,
                                               flower

of her I lived with half that year
love does not come by intention, even the lost tries
trying to give space — let it be —

the threads of its back
the threads of our nerves
strung and not let up
fuck into the dark hole over which
the one last nerve between us strung
lapses or straughts — straightens, taut —
breaks in two and snaps back on the bedstead
the sweat sopped into the sheets
into the mattress
                    and that flowers too, another florescence
                                               altogether

and the fuck of us
both is in the body's memory
cells of the hands, tits, cock and ass

is five feet out there in the air
that remembering

                    *

I wish we had fucked in the street

or in the bathroom, standing on my head
eating you sitting down, legs spread, my cock
in your mouth, legs across your shoulders

*

The flowers are in the street to come up or for us to wander in
the streets should be left open to all people, the meadows flowered
ways into sunlight or the dappled shade
once creek beds to play in, now these streets

marching to Oakland in the half fall light
                                one tendril
singing on a dark porch in the summer night sidestreet
                                one tendril
turning the corner crossing the street at the sight of a friend
                                one tendril

the flower that blooms out this window
can only bloom in the street if we walk there, each footstep
planted opens land beneath

those who walk in the middle of the street
        are completely different people than those who walk on
                                the sidewalk

and what was only in the dark before
        now moves in incessant colored movement
        down the intense sunlight

the flowers are *here* and *now*
        either there is one where you are
        or the space of you lacks you

I have come into the room, and weeds

Your life and your death are with your neighbor

and the sexual act in the street
        or on the bathroom floor
        goes on out of us, way past us
        till we can see it without any us in it at all

*

Your car sits in the half-moon outside
one tire flat, where you left it a night ago
We have been apart now half the months
we lived together
The hills above Berkeley
hang in the moonlight
the wind carries over the hills
as if the smell of calm
the summer night might bring
But I look up and out
and only the streetlights glare between me
and the dark rise beyond —
it is winter, and they
are cold as winter beyond this mild clime
Not that we long for each other now or want us back, pining,
but that we made it together —
calms, leaves the inner organs
eased to come again,
as calm, eyes shining and the hair,
as this light, as the rise of land
and fall, beyond the eyes
toward morning

12 Jan 65

LET THIS TIME HAVE ITS CANTO

— ROBERT DUNCAN

Toward Oakland in the night streetlight glare
the open ends of cars go by,
kids, highschool kids, it's Friday night
and in some distance the diffusion gives no direction of
a basketball game lets out, waves
here to the backporch wash on

                                 They and their cars
are flowers in the streets —
                           and from this notebook, my own
                                        petals
drift, fit to their own —
                       We will be calm
or we will be gassers — *the Beatles are gear*
written in passing
on a billboard

                      thrown open

flowers, flowers of us, flowers because
we open in the air

*

The fuck we all get tonight, or think about
incessantly, goes past us, is always more
than we are in it —
                    that is why
we enter it again and again, keep coming back, never tired
to make it again and again —
                      that is why
we go off in the streets,
                  drive and ride,

sing this song and shout, shake
it on out and stomp about

51

But the last line is not
where the record ends, or where
the car's broke down and the wheels fall off

                                baby

        it is so quiet the cars go by   like harps
                or guitars blown hard through
        even stars fall down and crinkle on the ground
        daddies
                        To *hear* each other, just to *hear*
        the other

        the songs we put over ourselves   because we're in them

        and then give up ourselves   into the others there

        sweet chops   pussy cat sweetie   hang loose

the last line is not anywhere we are not willing for it to be

                                        14 Jan 66

The flesh of the woman
idealized in childhood
without knowing, idealized and wanted
after in highschool, without ease
O her flesh. The dark brown
dirt under the fingernails
She was not idealized. She was
unknown country to come into
Men fuck women
to go beyond themselves, utterly, out
into that night or such heady light
nothing is known at all. Feeling the way
Men fuck men
to know them, to
sensuality of oneself
to communality, walking off together
across the near plains. The flesh is very near
Only rarely can men
endure the presence of gods

22 Jan 66

RICHLAND CEMETERY, WAKARUSA TOWNSHIP,
DOUGLAS COUNTY, KANSAS

the poetry of accomplishment   the reckoning of attaining
fierce reputation   vowels, muscles in sunlight
dead inchoate   restless compassion into contemplation
what union here   what ease is possible   what exaltation

beyond the yellow broomgrass   Blasdel turns his camera
toward where we talk   away from the gravestones
the sky smoky into spring   the green rising in us

the goods that can be held   without possession
the leap of mind   without compulsion
where the intellect sparkles   the grass rustles

late afternoon   toward Happy Valley
wondering of the land   to live on   to come to

the leap of body to its knowing

10 Mar 66

The hills beyond Lecompton west
rest as Virginia, mountains, Tennessee, alone
the farmyard driven to, wrong road taken
a dozen dogs run up, barking

mash smell almost in the air
the river working at the hills' edges
the flat flood plain half a mile wide
left into the valleys roads do not end

16 Mar 66

The road to the cliffs at Bodega Head
is grown back to grass again
There are no differences among us
as we walk back from the sea — green
fly us against the wind

Along the San Andreas fault
the poppies furled are on the verge
of opening — green
bend against the wind

There is no speech equivalent
to the distance crossed

But this

20 Mar 66

THREE GEOGRAPHICAL VARIATIONS

(FOR ED DORN)

North out of Lawrence we turned
east before we had to a back
track to Valley Falls and Ozawkie back
roads north into Hiawatha
Old trips of the past will not save us
Noon meals in or out of a calendar
picture quiet and readdress the east
turn into White Cloud and Iowa Point
to reach toward the river and where
the river's urge in us eased us a little
That is the flow the urge toward
each other links hand in hand as
word in word driving drinking beer all Sunday afternoon
I have come west and at the far ocean remember
It does not matter loose specifics of whose
the linkage matters the flow
the closeness possible the intimations of divinity
as intimations of the dreamed spread land
spread before the eyes of those White Clouds diddled sooners
even the willful wily promoters
looking west at the land's run
out from under them

*

I will not let blood and I do not know
if there is any turning back upon the land
to traverse, how much
traversing now will reopen
what spaces seem nowhere
ease us together — it is not different to go past
the endless misuse of landscape
here in Berkeley or there in New Mexico, what space
is open beyond is open across the whole world
Looks past whatever salvations of individuals
realizing salvation is only to pass
into the space all people live in

*

There is no need to substitute any world for this one
in order to come into any wonder or more
enter the open imagination. Good and evil
seem kindness and indifference   at each footstep
At the other edge of each tree   another pasture
the shade fallen on each face into the sun
Into each lit house dark street we walk home
The stories where we are all changed
beyond the wardrobe's back wall   pass through
The eye is blue wonder brown opener the horizon
shines through upon the toss and fling the ring glints
head up in the air   grass goes by   like starlings
iridescent in the sky

16 Apr 66

blackheaded grosbeaks in the box elder
toward Jemez the high clouds linger
over the river and drift on —
that is all blue in the distance, haze
as the hand lifted to shade to gaze
out from the sunlit terrace —
close at hand the silver salt bush
and across the red dun hills green
dots into gray of scrub juniper
aroma where the fingers crush it lingers
fingers run through the hair leave on the hair
the pomade of such wandering around
chiggers on the ankles bite to

*

the sunlight is in a thin line along the river valley, the high
stepped bluffs along the west stretches
highlighted, the fall of eyes to light
as naturally, looking idly up and down the blued haze stretches
north into the Jemez — all mountains and all ground
grown luminous behind the clouds and shadows, light
beneath and in all landscapes seen, whatever size —
down to these stones under the feet, leaves and samaras
blown across the table, box elder bugs
spin in quadrilaterals above the road
as in circles earlier today, before the rain, gray Canada jays
wheeled settling and rising on, moving eastward
through the gap toward Golden

*

the light falls across the room from my friend's lamp
gone to bed in the other room he sleeps or tosses around
                                             half-asleep
under the fall of the light here, the record going on the
                                             phonograph —
come to visit after two years almost — it is
into the light night air all goes, our
touching hands again, my staying here, the long

disjointed conversations — into the land's light, the dust
blown up in circles before the rain again tonight
the gnats in disjointed turns over the terrace — the light
that comes up from within the land
and down to us, part of it, from the sky

way north there are faint lights in the river valley, a few
where Los Alamos sits against the Jemez, faint
lines of snow on the peaks above Santa Fe
shine in the moonlight — behind us, out of sight
the tv towers on the crest blink red and off
as the heart beats and relaxes

*

apricot nectar, a flour can full of peyote buttons in the kitchen

*

the old what few songs few ever sang less sing now
late at night, one man, walking home, drunk, against
the dust rising from his footsteps, against one
fence and then the other, sings a Mexican
borracho song heard first a dozen years ago my brother
brought back from Mexico
78s scratched with dust

they fill, his phrases out of the song's
disjointed, as his laughing, stumbles
kick the knees out dancing down the road
poorwills churble in the piñon off the highway
swoop the small nighthawks by the cottonwoods off the hill

threads of an old song tie together
as string ties together his shirt falling apart

Martin sits crocked in the Thunderbird telling
how to work off too many hot chiles
's to get on a woman and work away and when you come
they're gone

riding home at 2 a.m., the moon
sets brick red toward Cabezon

29 May - 1 Jun 66

POINT REYES POEM

The fog moves in across the bay in combers strain out the sunlight

*

We climbed the path to Mt. Wittenberg on a clear Sunday
over the ocean the low clouds moved away from us
Reyes' spread hills spread away on every side
the sea into burned so bright we couldn't look straight at

The path to the sea
goes down gradually
miles of forest, onto
grasslands, let down
to empty farms, the steep
last hill, the pastures
flat a hundred yards
along the cliffs

The grass rises and burns
light, back lit and side
in the last light hours
lupine in, paint brush
slides a little, rides back up
the wind down the trees' gap
fans

*

There are only two ways onto the beach or back up
one down a stream's gully, steps cut, boards back up
the other through a blow hole, another stream's fall to

            caught us
ankle deep coming through from the sea side
tide up, wave backed
up the pants, sopped and socks squished in the boots

we stopped over the cliff rise to wring the socks out
poppies like earrings in the grass, over the cliff's edge toward China

*

The trail back is a road left over from the dairy farms, so gradual
no rise is felt at all, through bay trees showing
eucalyptus on the hills showing the sky in scattered patches
                                        white beyond

As we turn into the first of meadows in a string before the
                                        trail's end
a boy and girl rise from the roadside and start on ahead of us
Debussy's *Syrinx* playing on her radio
our dog in gazelled leaps chases deer along the hills above them

having come to the last meadow
        seven deer in three families move contrarywise in short
                                        directions grazing

having come to this meadow
        there is only the uncertainty of all purpose

*

And drove on, fog dark, sun set, north
        into the coast hills and redwoods
to Occidental, "wide place in the road
        with three enormous Italian restaurants"
fivecourse duck dinners, stuffed before the duck ever came
        rolling pebbles from the beach around on the table
offering to pay the waitress the final odd dollar due
        in quartz white stones

*

Frozen seafoam, petrified jellyfish
purpose but to wander, too rarely here, too often
mind in, locked gaze out
onto the splendiferous —
        as here the spread coniferous forest

o city, where all our meeting is —
not what buildings we have built
but where we always live

*

And with the duck in us head back —
        across the swamp flats below Napa
the lights in the bay float and waver
        "Goddam, coming through Sonoma
just to see the square"
        the black dog in the back seat shifts
cars mesh and pass   the radio light rises and floats
        into the directions home

over the Berkeley hills eucalyptus sway in the breeze
wind carries the smell of miles down wind, over the
                                        oceanbound air

*

Now in this room weeks later dill weed smells up the air
the rug's meadow light falls across —
                                room of the world
this is the room the eyes start out from
birds fly through the look on out
as gnats and flies fly through the room here

*

The space between the trees we enter holds us
the calm, light down into, over eucalyptus boughs
        the point the afternoon has met us
and we stop, the sound of our feet in the leaves
        leaving its echo past the ears

so we have brought our meeting with us
        carried as one room of air around us
to these trees

and suddenly stopped into the light
they merge, all spaces merge and fall away around us

o enter the splendid city!
            where all our meeting lies

28 Jul - 28 Aug 66

OUR CONVERSATION IS IN HEAVEN

— ST. PAUL

The friend who came to dinner has gone home
late night the streets full of sycamores holds all the spaces
held in our speaking — the conversation in the room
gone into the yard's opening, the long now pauses
between the phrases remembered, the alterations of cells
the body's answerings, long off echoes felt halfway to speaking

farting getting up to go upstairs to bed

New Jersey stretches away all trees out the attic window
only able to see the streetcorner's lights
only nearby, scattered up through the leaves
shifting slightly in endlessly connecting directions

as all the turns, half bits of thoughts started
abrupt, talking to John tonight, Jim and Angela
held and encountered, relaxed and begun again
laughing out in the middle of the living room

the light would break in all the windows of the house
if we looked at it once, would break in our eyes like window panes

that as we turn disjointed and uncertain
at even the next word, to make any connection
connects everything

11 Sep 66

There is only one world, and it is everywhere around us

    *

The fog in the trees drips,
                  over the hills
and far away the sun in the valley
shines where the snows above in the Sierras
rest early

We are not at home if we are not at rest
going and coming in —
                  home is the bed's
stead, where the rest takes place
all the circulations, out and in
that lead to sleep at last and back, to calm

as   drip   drip
calms the traffic's sounds
into their own and granted, widening orders

    *

That is the incessant writhing movement
we have seen upon the walls

the light in the dark parts of the house
that does not ever leave us
eyes closed or gone into this dream's
other dream, 's sleep

careful of us You are

we have seen that care
move with us everywhere

till it is even brought to face the contorted hatreds of misorder
        their own misnomers
faced across the table or across the interval of sidewalk
drafts, armies, police of imposition
impossible offices of even the most benign appearance
        hateful

only the human, the human is broken
in them

where even on *their* faces swirl
the endless curves and revelations of the light

Wrath is the breaking down of all relation

*

That would be anyone met in the forests of these hills and fog
not known before, only this meeting
the possible transcendence of all preconceptions
and the self given over out of isolation

now, only now, *now*
                              the   drip
        drip   of the fog
                                counting
        this eternity

*

The green man covered with his vines beneath his suit
around the corner of Cragmont Park toward the fall of rock away
we said only a few words, looking out toward the bay
where the words met in the space around us
dark tendrils in us grow carried in us now
        out toward the space, who comes toward me

is not the same space, changed, she comes from blossoms from
                                          the grass
        across July, Tilden Park a hill once, or
        Shattuck and Vine, her flowers from her hair
        in the laundromat, halfway into evening, leaning
        against the change machine, the odors of us
        mixed and smiled at in the air, we knew them

        flowers, flowers of us

CERVE

you who pass through this poem
and out the other side
                                        counted

by the eternity
of the words

*

They would have us forget the eternity of the music
that the music is there at all

they would have us only be angry at them
or be quiet in desperation, submission in no other terms
than theirs

not *hear* the music, the flow of all movement

*

The sun has set squarely in the Golden Gate
into the bed of clouds come up just before

We are the last first people, Olson said
and this is our West, the *cloud-capp'd . . . palaces*
left *not a rack behind* —
but recognizing that lost, this ungot-at and still held, West
over and over again in these sunsets
these vistas, this down and home again to ocean, start
up and never seen before province
revealed its inner lights no clearer time than sunset
can we see where we are before us

come to this ocean and this gate
the clouds give name to
silence is golden

*

The friends that did not come, the enemies

that did and not known to come upon
new land come into —
                              this old swell of elegance, San Francisco
the assuager of all such loss and loneliness
or dust washed off and liquor made in place of water
as if the gold were
in the liquid

movement of the eyes

*

Ravagement. War gone on
abroad far west of here and with no
vision of the light across us, we are in, but
spilt blood's light

Already in Vaughn Moody's time
his soldier face down in the sand in the Philippines
An Ode in Time of Hesitation
is clear now has been
uninterruptedly hesitated upon
to this, no longer hesitant, full given, plunge into
        darkness

dark at the heart of the nation
that has no other light to see by but spilt blood's

But the city, Charles Williams said,
we can found, at any moment —
the nation can only appear

and what the city is
        between us
is as we choose and let loose
from our sluices of the divine
what pitches and currents caught in us
cross to the person
facing or turned even part way

toward us

the sunset in the air
as our light in the air
between us

*

And the music flows
that out of this unknown country into the sunset ruled it all
overcomes, regulates into another order
the ravagement made
out of tossed up and not kept promises
— inhabitants and use of land —
out of unsaid, held in, secret, and most kept promises
        with only inward gods

But the music, the music!
I *hear* you, I *hear* you
said against all fears of paranoia
to the person across from us

Sam across from me in a bar in Torreon
half a decade back
thinking I was putting him down
I pleaded not to turn away
away from the spread out top of table's
place where all our meeting lay
not back, into the lost
dark self's involvement
no place touches onto

and he is gone now from me, I from him
but in regret and rancor, ravagement

Bound upon the wheel
as we are, the lama
said to Kim, be not
angry with the man, for he

has already repented, and you
have only a Red Mist
before your eyes. Let it
wash away in the River
that we all seek

*

But the meeting once held
is not ever gone or let forgotten
The love held and acknowledged
the fire flow of each person
letting through him the fire flow
of all movement

still vital in the air
the cells of the body changed by it
permanently

as against such transformation
the ravages against the light
wear down the body
clog up the sluices through

*

Sam, I have learned to love with you
and not expect return, know
the love flows on unimpeded
given back or not
but loosed —
                    and that there is no
seeing the returning, your holding of the heart
's movement beyond yourself
— that is always love —
hidden from my
foil-ridden, sunset and tree-within
ridden mind

*

There is only one world, and it is everywhere around us

5-6 Nov 66

STRIKE (UC BERKELEY, DECEMBER 1966)

All that is unjust leaves us impatient with eternity.

— ROBERT DUNCAN

Vaughan saw Eternity in a great ring of light in the heavens. I
have seen it this afternoon in the swirling fog through the trees
and houses on the hills above Berkeley — looking out the great
east window of the library reference room, the strike on, thou-
sands standing in the rain in the plaza at noon. Only as we are
at ease to move among each other, as the rain and fog move
among us, are we free. The place from which we move toward
Eternity, move to perception at all, depends for its being open on
our acts between us.

*

Now as the rain gusts west, wind out of the valley
toward the open sea
                                        the dull gray in the brains of men
blows leafless, stuck in the mud

Strawberry Creek rages bank-full and brown
west as well, we who are anchored
                                        only by our feet
wander to intents as well as these

*

Protesting the use of the campus
given freely and with all commitment
to recruit Navy for the war
when other nonstudents, protestors of the war, had been denied

students sat down around the Navy's table
rather than leave that crux of use
loose, fluxed and wishy-washy washed away
in the old loosed promises
lap, the Navy breaks over and over in those waters
only that much war away

you can make such references in history
but in literature it is not so easy

Cheat asked for "imaginative and creative proposals"
and then rejected corridors of access offered through the human
community of space made on the floor around the doors to
                                      the Union bookstore
the human aisles the doors to the true union

proclaimed a riot in the midst of singing
and called the Alameda County cops and had them
pick out the 9 nonstudents as alleged only leaders

sometimes the same reference will serve —
such as personal names, and geographic names,
and names of corporate bodies

the use of *imagination,* the act of *creation*
being the wielding of inarticulate and sense-less
(having no means to sense but)
strongarm power

all references to this place
      are to all places
all references to these names
      are to all people
and this corporate body
      to all institutings of power
above the relation between each person and each person

censorship is the effort to — or the actual prohibition
                                of communication

*

Streams out of us, words, acts in silence, singing
from the land under foot
from the common land held inside us
Strawberry Creek carrying to the Pacific tides
        these silts and erosions
the war west of here 10,000 miles receives slowly
but inevitably the directions of our weather

*

STRIKE   COPS ON CAMPUS

DON'T GO TO CLASS   GO TO THE LIBRARY AND STUDY

MAN THE PICKET LINES

the leaflets drawn hastily and printed overnight
        a student being dragged off by a cop with
        arm raised wielding the campanile as a club

keep time in hand
and beat those down
who seek what smidgen even
        of eternity, justice
to see it by

or say it is not time

*We are told that unless Heyns gets faculty support . . . then
Somebody Worse will take his place. . . Somebody Worse is in
Sproul Hall right now.*

the *time* is not right
                    ripe, fall off the tree and rot
                    before ready?

too *young* to make such decisions
                                STRIKE
and answer now an emptiness
between the strokes of the campanile
as opening and limitless

*

The rain is so heavy in gusts umbrellas are flipped inside out
and the cover brought against the direct weather
is blown away

the picketers at the end of Telegraph
circle the center the restless movement up and down the avenue
leads to

at the point you look at the center
into the rain and fog beyond
at the point the center of the look is
each person at each person passing
eyes now up directly to eyes
every face is the surface on which we *see* the light
STRIKE against the dull gray in the mind SPARK
HERE held out in the eyes held out in the eyes' look back

*

Face the rains again, falling to flood
all night on new asphalt
up washing clothes past midnight
in a laundromat on University

the revolution will go on
whatever suppression of this attempt
kept in the active underground
and passed on to each new year of students

*

The strike over, voted out of fear down by an old academy
                                                    of faculty
and the threats made, better never do it again
the conditions from which all discontent grew, no different
only the threat clearer, unequivocal the lines drawn
solidified, the stick up the ass of power

if it is not here now it will be here again
the names of *California* and *university*
gone on into another relevance than guessed at first

every day the struggle:

let not the given conditions of each day
drag down the first moment of waking
and keep dragged
no goods finally ever enough
even when the few goods got are got

— no, not even this exhortation —

if we *see* each other
we make an eternity
in the weather

Light is the result, the rubbed two sticks
of all relation

1-8 Dec 66

US NO1 FANCY
CALROSE RICE
GOLDEN STATE
BRAND
POETS CHIOS
ALL OTHER WORLDS
48 ‹ As a man is, so he sees. As the
Eye is formed, such are its powers 7 49
—WM. BLAKE

*Printed March 1970 in Santa Barbara by
Noel Young for the Black Sparrow Press.
Design by Barbara Martin. This edition is
limited to 600 copies in paper wrappers;
175 hardbound copies numbered & signed by
the poet; & 26 lettered copies handbound
in boards by Earle Gray, each signed & with
an original illustration by the poet.*